Child labour: A guide to project design

Child labour: A guide to project design

Alec Fyfe

International Labour Office   Geneva

Fyfe, A.
Child labour: A guide to project design. ILO Child Labour Collection
Geneva, International Labour Office, 1993

/Manual/, /Project design/, /Child labour/, 01.01.6
ISBN 92-2-108005-6

ILO Cataloguing in Publication Data

The designations employed in ILO publications, which are in conformity with United Nations practice, and the presentation of material therein do not imply the expression of any opinion whatsoever on the part of the International Labour Office concerning the status of any country, area or territory or of its authorities, or concerning the delimitation of its frontiers. The responsibility for opinions expressed in signed articles, studies and other contributions rests solely with the authors, and publication does not constitute an endorsement by the International Labour Office of the opinions expressed in them. Reference to names of firms and commercial products and processes does not imply their endorsement by the International Labour Office, and any failure to mention a particular firm, commercial product or process is not a sign of disapproval.

ILO publications can be obtained through major booksellers of ILO local offices in many countries, or direct from ILO Publications, International Labour Office, CH-1211 Geneva 22, Switzerland. A catalogue or list of new publications will be sent free of charge from the above address.

Printed in Switzerland   ATA

Foreword

The last few years have witnessed a major shift in attitude, and the emergence of positive developments and opportunities at both national and international levels, in the campaign against child labour. The persistence of child labour under abusive and exploitative conditions is attracting far more attention than ever before, both as a response to the ILO's work and as part of a worldwide movement associated with the United Nations Convention on the Rights of the Child (1989) and the World Summit on Children (1990). Member States are increasingly interested in taking practical action against child labour, and more and more governments are approaching the ILO for technical assistance. Significantly also, practical small-scale projects concerned with working children are being undertaken in growing numbers in Africa, Asia and Latin America, notably and overwhelmingly by non-governmental organizations. These projects vary in size and scope. Many, and in fact most, are aimed at providing various kinds of protective services such as non-formal education, vocational training, health, nutrition and even shelter for working and street children. Others focus on advocacy, public awareness and mobilization with a view to exerting pressure on governments to protect the welfare and the rights of children.

Many of these projects are financed through individual contributions, but as many or more rely on assistance from governments and external donors. Financing agencies of course insist that projects be carefully designed so as to provide transparency, especially as to the relationship between goals, activities, outputs and inputs, and to facilitate implementation and evaluation. Hence this manual has been written, the first of its kind on child labour, I believe.

We hope that it will provide a practical tool for governmental and non-governmental organizations alike in the design of more effective responses to protecting and assisting working children.

The preparation of this manual has involved a number of units and colleagues in the Office, and I should therefore like to express my appreciation to the various colleagues in the Conditions of Work and Welfare Facilities Branch and the Evaluation Unit for their interest and assistance. I should especially like to thank Claude Dumont under whose responsibility this idea was first launched and who was closely involved at all stages. Enrique Brú, Nelien Haspels and Jan Versluis were most helpful in sharing with us their extensive experience and expertise in project design and evaluation, and were involved right from the beginning in the conceptualization and drafting of this manual. Their contribution was invaluable.

Assefa Bequele
Project Manager
Interdepartmental Project on the Elimination of Child Labour,
Working Conditions and Environment Department

Sources and acknowledgments

A number of existing project design manuals were consulted in the course of drafting this publication. Of particular assistance was the simplified version of the 1981 ILO manual, *How to write a project document*.

The matrix developed by Bill Myers, as set out in Box One, was used for conceptualizing projects for working children, and his *Protecting working children* (London and New Jersey, Zed Books/UNICEF, 1991) was a general inspiration. The concept of quality criteria in project appraisal was derived from a 1991 reference paper, *The theory and practice of the appraisal of technical co-operation projects*, produced by the UNIDO Secretariat for an expert group meeting held in Vienna in September 1991. Randal Joy Thompson's paper, "Conducting fourth generation evaluations: The art of construction and negotiation", in *AID Evaluation News*, 1991, was most helpful in presenting trends in the field. The work of Robert Chambers was invaluable for the discussion of rapid appraisal techniques. UNICEF's *Methodological guide on situation analysis of children in especially difficult circumstances* (Bogotá, 1988) was a seminal text for Chapters 7, 8 and 9.

Contents

9. The effects of work on children: A checklist

10. Summary and checklist on how to write a a project document

List of figures

List of boxes

Introduction

This manual offers a set of guiding principles, combined with a variety of practical tools. It aims to help the practitioner in non-governmental and governmental agencies involved in combating child labour design projects and draft project documents for the benefit of working children.

The manual is divided into three parts.

Part I provides the background and context to project design. *Chapter 1* gives an overview of the extent and consequences of child labour, and responses to it. *Chapter 2* places projects in the broader context of policies and programmes.

Part II follows a step-by-step approach to project design using the *logical framework* format, which is well established in the development field. *Chapter 3* explains the first set of key elements, concerned with defining *the problem, the strategy, the target groups* and *the partners*. The second set of key elements of a project are explored in *Chapter 4*. These are *objectives, outputs, activities and inputs*, which have to be closely linked together if a project is to make sense. The chapter concludes with the last group of project components — *indicators, assumptions* and *preconditions*. *Chapter 5* rounds off Part II with an examination of the processes of *monitoring* and *evaluation*. These often get overlooked, but they provide vital feedback into project design.

1

Part III addresses the question: *"How do we do it?"* This section of the manual provides practical tools. *Chapter 6* presents the first of these tools, which are the key international labour standards relating to child labour. As so much depends on the ability to conduct quality investigations into child labour, two chapters deal with this issue. *Chapter 7* gives guidance on how to conduct *problem* or *situation analysis*. This requires the ability to understand and use a variety of methods: *secondary sources; observation; surveys;* and *interviews*. *Chapter 8* takes the most widely used of these methods — *interviews* — and offers guidance on the "do's" and "don'ts" of interviewing. *Chapter 9* provides a checklist for examining the effects of work on children. *Chapter 10* is a summary of Part II: it provides a brief guide on how to write a project document and finally gives a checklist to help you make sure that your project document is clear, complete and consistent.

Finally, it must be stressed *that the manual provides an enabling framework and not a blueprint* that must be rigidly applied. It must be adapted to your circumstances and needs.

PART I

BACKGROUND AND CONTEXT

1. Child labour: An overview

1.1. Working children and the international community

C hild labour remains one of the most neglected human rights issues of our time. The recently adopted United Nations Convention on the Rights of the Child (1989) affirms the right of children to education, self-expression and freedom from exploitative work. Children are not little adults — their fundamental right is to childhood itself.

The first priority of the ILO is the promotion of social justice, including human rights and the implementation of international labour standards. Nowhere are these two aims better united than in the quest to eliminate child labour. Indeed the abolition of child labour was one of the guiding principles of the ILO's Constitution in 1919, and it remains one of its chief goals.

The principal means of action has been the setting of international labour standards. The ILO Conventions have had a significant influence nationally and internationally, and most have been incorporated in national legislation. But, as so often happens, the gap between principle and practice can become a chasm. Millions of children currently fall victim to this failure to implement minimum age legislation and provide universal schooling.

1.2. The global situation

C hild labour is the major cause of child abuse and exploitation in many parts of the world. No one knows for certain how many children are working. Much child work is illegal, and there is often an attempt to conceal it. Africa has the highest proportion in the world of working children (nearly one-third), whilst Latin America, with its high levels of urbanization, has the largest population of "street children". And in many Asian countries children comprise over 10 per cent of the workforce. Given the problems of the world economy in the 1980s, there can be no grounds for complacency that child labour has diminished in many countries; in the 1990s the problem is more likely to persist or worsen.

1.3. What is child labour?

D efining child labour is not as simple and straightforward as it may appear because it encompasses three difficult-to-define concepts: *"child"*, *"work"*, and *"labour"*. Childhood can be defined in terms of age, but then different societies may have different thresholds for demarcating childhood and adulthood. In some societies, age may not be a sufficient basis for defining "childhood". The fulfilment of certain social rites and traditional obligations may well be important requirements in defining "adult" and "child" status. In still others, the integration of children into socio-economic life may begin so early, and the transition from childhood to adulthood may be so smooth and gradual, that it may be virtually impossible to identify clearly the different life phases. We must therefore recognize that we are dealing with a concept which could mean different things depending on the context. Besides, in the absence of an effective age record system, even applying an agreed legal definition becomes highly problematic.

However, in the context of child labour, a working definition of a "child" may be a person below the general limit of 15 years or in special circumstances 14 years, set by the Minimum Age Convention, 1973 (No. 138). A fuller treatment of Convention No. 138 is given in Chapter 6.

Very often children work because they and their families are poor. But poverty is not always the cause of child labour. There are also cultural pressures — particularly on girls. Employers too may simply view children as the cheapest form of labour on the market. And there are also extreme cases, such as child forced labour. Particularly vulnerable to exploitation are children from ethnic minority, low-income and low-class groups, and girls.

One reason for the general lack of attention given to the problem in the past is the perceived difficulty of distinguishing between positive and negative child work. There are, after all, strong common-sense, cultural, economic and educational reasons to support the widely held view that work can be positive for children. Through work children can gain increasing status as family members and citizens. They can learn the skills of their parents and neighbours. Work can therefore build their confidence and self-esteem, and can be a painless and gradual initiation into adult life. In practice many children work, and from an early age of 6 or 7, often on a family farm. Work can clearly be a positive influence on child development. So why is *child labour* often seen as negative?

The problem is that when the conditions of work change, the picture changes dramatically. Work turns into exploitation when children:

— *work too young:* many children start factory work at 6 or 7 years, for example in the carpet industry;

— *work too long hours:* in some cases 12-16 hours a day;

— *work for too little pay:* as little as $3 for a 60-hour week or no pay, as in agriculture;

— *work in hazardous conditions:* in mines, quarries, plantations, sweatshops or even on the streets;

— *work under slave-like arrangements:* there are an estimated 20 million child bonded labourers in South Asia.

1.4. Responses

The legislative approach

When reformers first began to respond to the problem of child labour over 150 years ago in industrialized countries, their strategy was to mobilize public opinion behind the demand for protective legislation. Indeed, in some cases during this period, children were protected by legislation before adult workers. Soon after the adoption of minimum age legislation (with a labour inspectorate to enforce it) came the second and more conclusive step — the introduction of universal education. Children were gradually, over many decades, removed from the farm and the factory to be placed in the classroom. This marked a revolution in societies' attitudes towards children, particularly of the role of the State in protecting children.

Today the most important and comprehensive international standard on minimum age is the Minimum Age Convention, 1973 (No. 138), which has been ratified by 40 countries (see Box Nine, p. 55). In fact most member States of the ILO have adopted a minimum age standard of 14 or higher, and more than 100 countries have ratified one or more of the ten minimum age Conventions prior to Convention No. 138.

But the legislative approach, though certainly necessary, is not sufficient to combat child labour. Coverage may be limited. Many national laws tend to exclude the informal sector and agriculture where most children work. Enforcement has always been problematic, even in industrialized countries. Legislation can also unintentionally make the situation worse, by driving child labour underground into the mushrooming unregulated sector, where detection, and therefore protection, are more difficult. It is therefore important to ensure that legislation is complemented by other reinforcing and complementary measures. We shall come back to this subject in Chapter 6, which gives a more detailed treatment of international labour standards.

Recent developments

Many policy, programme and project designers recognize that child labour cannot be legislated out of existence overnight. Abolition remains the long-term goal, but children need protection here and now. The switch has been from purism to pragmatism, with an emphasis on a broad range of practical measures in a number of areas. These include: education and training; advocacy and public awareness raising; welfare provision; protected work schemes; regulation and enforcement.

Of these, education and training are the key instruments. Education laws are the best laws against child labour and they are often much easier to enforce.

Non-governmental organizations (NGOs) have provided most of the response to, and experimentation in, child labour. But child labour demands the political will and resources which only governments can provide, coupled with the unrivalled capacity of voluntary organizations to work at the community level. Only then will policies, programmes and projects be enhanced to the benefit of working children.

CHAPTER SUMMARY

Question	Answer
What is a child?	Different laws have set varying age limits for the determination of what is a child. In conjunction with "labour", ILO Convention No. 138 places the general limit at 15 years or, under special national circumstances, 14 years.
What is child labour?	This is child work which is exploitative and threatens the health, welfare and development of children.
What is the single most important remedy?	Education and training. But parents must be able to afford this, and of course schooling must be made available.

2. Policies, programmes and projects

There is often a tendency to confuse the terms "policies", "programmes" and "projects". They are, and should be of course, closely linked, but it is important to define them clearly so that we develop a rounded and strategic view of actions needed to eliminate child labour and if we are to properly set the context for project design.

2.1. Policies

A policy on child labour is a public commitment to work towards the elimination of child labour, setting out objectives and priorities, coupled with the resource provision to ensure implementation.

There can never be a substitute for a policy commitment from governments to the long-term goal of elimination of child labour, coupled with short-term measures which protect working children. Here the Minimum Age Convention, 1973 (No. 138), along with its companion Recommendation, 1973 (No. 146), provides guidance to governments in framing national policies and programmes. Both suggest priorities for all countries:

— the identification and prohibition of child work in hazardous activities;

— the protection of the youngest and most vulnerable children, i.e. those under 12 years of age.

Whatever the level of development of the country, the first and foremost priority should be the identification and prohibition of hazardous work, to be found both in agriculture and in urban-based industries. Allied to this public policy goal should be an emphasis upon the protection of the youngest and most vulnerable children. This could be accomplished by ensuring compulsory primary education to the age of 12 or 13 years.

Child labour is often caused by poverty. But this is only part of the truth, and should never be grounds for doing nothing. Many flagrant and extreme abuses, such as bonded labour, could be abolished relatively quickly, if the necessary political will existed.

2.2. Programmes

P olicies are the first step. They have to be implemented through programmes — a comprehensive and coherent set of interventions in such areas as:

— *education and training;*

— *welfare services;*

— *protected work schemes;*

— *advocacy/public-awareness raising;*

— *regulation and enforcement.*

A programme approach requires that the various social ministries (labour, education, health and welfare) devise effective machinery for cooperation and coordination. Indeed, such institutional arrangements, e.g. the setting up of child labour units, are essential if child labour is to be placed on the public policy agenda. Here the Ministry of Labour, given its mandate, ought to take a leading role.

2.3. Projects

P rojects are the building blocks of programmes. They are more limited in scope and time. A project may often work with one target group, in a particular sector, using one or a limited range of interventions, over a period of two to three years.

Projects address a wide variety of concerns. They usually focus on certain target groups such as children engaged in rural work, match and fireworks production, carpet-making, construction, rag-picking, collection and recycling of assorted waste products, and work in quarries. They also include sexually abused children, migrant children, shoeshine and parking boys, children in domestic service and self-employed boys and girls. They vary in terms of objectives or types of activity undertaken. Some provide a range of welfare services such as nutrition and health care to alleviate the hardships at work. Others develop skills, carry out advocacy campaigns and support the strengthening of organizational capacity. Still others promote schooling by providing special support for children from poor families, such as stipends and nutrition, and some use public information campaigns and other measures to combat child employment in highly exploitative and hazardous conditions.

Two of the most promising examples of efforts at the project or grass-roots level are those concerned with access to education and training, and those whose primary objective is the provision of protected work and income-earning opportunities.

In Box One we have provided a typology of child labour projects in terms of the possible types and levels of intervention.

In the field of child labour a comprehensive approach would involve at least *five types of intervention:* education and training; welfare services; protected work; advocacy; and regulation and enforcement. These interventions would further need to be applied at *four principal levels in society:* the child; the family; the community; and the government.

The typology may assist you in designing your project by helping you to identify the best starting point. It may also provide governmental and non-governmental organizations alike with a means of finding out what is the present response to child labour, and what still needs to be done in order to build a comprehensive national programme.

Of course this model is an ideal in terms of the lines and levels of action which it proposes. This is not to suggest that all these elements should feature in a particular project or programme; no one institution

13

Box One

A TYPOLOGY OF CHILD LABOUR PROJECTS

Type of intervention	Levels of intervention			
	Child	Family	Community	Government
Education and training	— Access to schooling — Non-formal education — Vocational training	— Stipends — Adapting school hours to family needs — Educating parents on value of education	— Provision of schooling and vocational training in community centres	— Expansion of education, especially universal primary education to be made compulsory — Reforms to promote access, especially for girls and those in rural areas
Welfare services	— Health monitoring — Supplementary nutrition — Access to health care — Removal from hazardous work	— Health education — Social security — Welfare support — Income generation	— Provision of community health centres — Drop-in centres	— Expansion of health and welfare provision based on community provision — Devolving power to local level
Protected work	— Provision of safe employment tailored to developmental needs		— Provision of protected work schemes — Volunteer support	— Government support of community-based initiatives

	— Work placement schemes — Sheltered workshops			
Advocacy	— Establish contact using peers — Developing awareness of situation and rights — Develop self-representation — Use of mass media, e.g. comics	— Information on health and education	— Citizens' groups — Community theatre — Mass media, e.g. radio — Mobilize teachers, religious groups, voluntary organizations, employers' groups	— Awareness-raising within ministries — Communicating strategies raising public awareness
Regulation and enforcement	— Raise awareness of labour laws — Report violations	— Educate families concerning the law and their responsibilities	— Mobilize trade unions on behalf of unorganized and marginal workers — Educate employers on the law and work effects on children — Citizens' committees and pressure groups for enforcement	— New legislation where necessary — Adaptation of laws to local reality — Expansion of inspectorate and its enhanced quality — Registration campaigns

or organization can do everything. *The greatest impact is likely to come from a cooperative approach between the public and private sectors.*

Stages in project development

All actions have four essential phases:

— defining and understanding the problem;

— planning a course of action;

— implementing the course of action;

— evaluating the effect and impact.

This is also a cyclical process because good project design leads to good evaluation, from which will emerge lessons to help improve existing projects and to formulate more effective projects in the future, and so on. Incorporating the lessons of evaluation into new project design turns the process into a spiral (figure 1).

Figure 1.   *The project development cycle: Responding; reviewing; planning and doing*

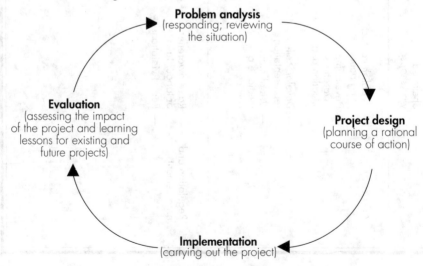

If we wish to set this process out in a linear step-by-step way, then we can identify the following *main stages in project development:*

1. *Identification* of the problem.
2. *Situation analysis* — finding out about the problem.
3. *Project design* — formulating a project document.
4. *Implementation* — carrying out the project.
5. *Monitoring* — checking on the progress of the project.
6. *Evaluation* — assessing whether the project met its aims.

What makes a good project?

— *Relevance.* A project may be both feasible and cost-effective but still may not be relevant because it fails to tackle the problem it set out to address.

— *Feasibility.* We need to know whether a project is likely to achieve its objectives — how realistic is it? Here it is important to know what risks the project faces and the nature and extent of its resources.

— *Cost-effectiveness.* We need to know the relationship between the costs of implementing a project and its expected benefits. When comparing different strategies for the same project or different projects, the best alternative is the one which achieves the expected objectives at a lower cost.

— *Sustainability.* The final test of an effective project is whether it can go on delivering benefits after external assistance has been withdrawn. Here it is important to avoid a common mistake among development workers — *it is not projects which should be sustained but their achievements*

2.4. Conclusions

P rojects are drops in the ocean given the growing magnitude of child labour. That is why all project designers need to view their contribution in a wider context. When it comes to community-level action, voluntary organizations have proved more adept at meeting the practical needs of working children. Indeed, the typical response to the problem of child labour over the last decade has been the NGO pilot project. Voluntary organizations nevertheless need to make connections, both with similar initiatives within the private sector and, more importantly, with programmes at the national level. *Governments can and must establish the climate, scope and framework for action*, whilst NGOs are particularly effective in developing community-level projects and the advocacy needed to complement these larger-scale activities. In the campaign to eliminate child labour, one of the key challenges remains how to combine the strengths of the public and private sectors to make the whole greater than the sum of its parts.

The contemporary picture is still one of largely experimental and fragmentary projects rather than a coherent set of programmes. Ministries fail to respond and coordinate. NGOs fail to network effectively. The whole is less than the sum of the parts. To move to a more developed stage means keeping to a common set of principles. And though projects cannot of themselves solve the problem of child labour, they are a good starting point. They help us to understand this complex issue, and show that practical action can be undertaken now.

CHAPTER SUMMARY

Policy	A public commitment to eliminate child labour in line with relevant international standards, which sets out objectives and priorities, coupled with the resource provision to ensure implementation.
Programme	A comprehensive and coherent set of projects or actions stemming from a policy commitment at the national level.
Project	An intervention, or set of interventions, more limited in scope, usually at the community level, and typically over the short term.
The project cycle	Make a commitment to respond to child labour; identify a problem; plan a rational course of action; carry out the project; monitor and evaluate the project; review the situation; extract lessons learned and plan a new project based on further needs; and start all over again, hopefully at a higher level of development.
Quality criteria	Is the project relevant? Is the project feasible, i.e. realistic? Is the project cost-effective? Are the project results sustainable, i.e. will activities continue after external funding has ended?
Approaches to child labour	A comprehensive strategy will operate at all *four levels of society:* the child — the family — the community — the government. It will also involve at least *five types of intervention:* education and training — welfare services — protected work — advocacy — regulation and enforcement.

PART II

THE LOGICAL FRAMEWORK APPROACH

3. Key elements in project design 1: Project rationale and strategy

3.1. Introduction

A well-designed project has a written document which is logical and complete. It is important to produce a project document because it:

— sets out a plan for what will be done, produced when and by whom;

— forms the basis for evaluation by describing the situation prior to the project and the objectives to be attained at the end of the project;

— establishes a contract, setting out the duties and responsibilities of each of the partners.

The aim of this and the following two chapters is to help you to understand the key design concepts and the linkages between them. Chapter 10 in Part III provides help in setting out these concepts in the format of a project document.

In order to make the writing up of a project document easier, the logical framework approach is divided into three manageable "packages". In this chapter we shall cover the package of elements which go together to form the *project strategy*, consisting of:

— *the problem;*
— *the target group;*

— *the partners;*

— *the approach* — *direct support (DS) or institutional development (ID).*

3.2. Identifying the problem

Perhaps one of the most difficult problems for a project designer is knowing where to begin and what questions to ask.

Child labour is a many-sided problem which requires a range of interventions. The project designer has to decide on a particular topic, and then start to identify key questions (Box Two).

Box Two

KEY QUESTIONS ON IDENTIFYING THE PROBLEM

WHY   is the project being undertaken?

WHAT is the particular aspect of child labour which gives rise to the project?

HOW   does the project fit into any local, regional or national programme?

HOW   does the project relate to priorities set out in international standards?

These initial questions help clarify the background and identify and define a problem, in concrete and specific terms, which justifies the project.

EXAMPLES:
In the State of Atlantis, some 15,000 boys and girls work as bonded labourers in the carpet industry, despite national legislation which outlaws it. These children suffer great deprivation and work in distant, isolated villages in largely unregistered premises. Child bonded labourers are over-

whelmingly from the most marginal ethnic minority groups with little or no experience of medical care or schooling. The processes of release and rehabilitation are problematic.

There is every danger that without adequate preparation, released child bonded labourers and their families will be forced back into dependency on local landowners, money-lenders, traders, etc. Special arrangements therefore need to be made for these children, particularly in the provision of education and training. With the closure of some of the largest factories in the State there is an urgent need to provide basic education and training for 3,000 boys and girls. This provides an excellent opportunity to undertake an experimental project in education and training.

The Government has recently developed a national policy on child labour and is undertaking a series of pilot projects within a range of industries with a high incidence of child workers. Many hundreds of thousands of children and their families are expected to benefit from these projects on a nationwide basis.

However, the programme has resulted in new and in-creased demands on the Ministry of Labour for leadership, technical assistance in designing, monitoring and evaluat-ing projects, training, and developing manuals, guidelines and checklists for project staff, experts and labour inspec-tors. In addition, the need to develop its policy and plan-ning capacity will become more acute when the Ministry of Labour transfers these projects to other regions not yet covered. Without enhanced capability, the significant gov-ernment investment may be underutilized, adversely affect-ing the whole programme.

More detailed advice on how to conduct problem analysis is given in Chapter 7 (Part III of the manual).

3.3. Project strategy

*T*he project strategy must make clear what you want to do, for whom, with whom and how. Having set out the reasons for undertaking the project, you now need to outline how the project will bring about beneficial changes and why it is designed in a particular way. It is up to the project designer to find the best way forward. Any project strategy is made up of a number of elements. Again we can start by asking key questions (Box Three).

BOX THREE

KEY QUESTIONS ON PROJECT STRATEGY

WHICH   group of child workers will benefit directly from the project?

WHICH   group of child workers will benefit indirectly from the project?

WHO   are the partners you will work with in helping the child workers?

WHAT   alternative project strategies have been considered, and why have they been rejected in favour of the one(s) chosen?

Who is to benefit? — The target group

One of the first things you want to know about a project is who is to benefit. In child labour projects, working children are naturally the *target group* or *intended beneficiaries*. Projects should be aimed at meeting their needs (Box Four).

It is important to define the target group precisely if the activities of the project are to be properly focused and if we are to answer the obvious question: "Did the project help the people it was supposed to help?" Here it is important to avoid vague general descriptions such as "street children". It is much better to give a precise size, location and social/economic/cultural characteristics of the target group. For example not all "street children", but: "Five hundred migrant children living with their peers, or in workplaces, in the city of Atlantis, without regular family contact."

Box Four

SELECTING AND INVOLVING THE TARGET GROUP

In selecting the target group it is important to recognize certain traditional biases in the field — those in favour of boys in "visible" activities like street trading, in an urban setting. Project designers need to counter these biases by selecting target beneficiaries from the "invisible" sectors such as domestic and agricultural work, where girls often predominate, or where low income or caste groups are the subject of the worst excesses of child labour, as in the case of bonded labour. Another bias that project designers need to guard against is the "top-down" approach which views working children and their families as passive products of the project process, rather than the active means of change. It is at this stage of defining the problem and project strategy that, wherever practicable, children themselves and their community should be consulted over the project design. Put simply: Do they want the project? Does it meet their needs? Is this the best possible strategy?

By involving them at this preparatory stage you not only avoid some very serious design pitfalls, but you also increase the chances of success by developing a sense of project ownership. Community participation is then an important feature of project design.

Project partners

Reaching children at risk demands collaboration between a range of agencies, both public and private. And given the scale of the problem it makes little sense if agencies compete over scarce resources. Only a partnership at local, national and global levels can hope to combat child labour effectively. A very important aspect of the project strategy is then the choosing of partners through which the project will work.

Projects should not be conceived in isolation, nor do they operate in a vacuum. How effective a project is will depend crucially on the relationships it forges with its target beneficiaries and partners. At a practical level this will require effective networking and coordination. If the project is, for example, an NGO/governmental organization partnership, it will be important to clarify roles and responsibilities in advance: Where are the lines of authority? What are the channels of communication? Do people have clear job descriptions? If the project is targeted at governments, then it is important that the various social ministries coordinate their efforts through, for instance, a child labour unit or similar mechanism.

It may be necessary to set up a project steering committee to coordinate the various partners involved in the project. These types of mechanism to ensure smooth project implementation are called *the institutional framework.*

How will the project deliver its benefits?

Having defined who are to benefit, you should also finally outline how they will benefit, i.e. the *project approach.* Here it is important to choose the most appropriate type and level of project intervention:

— assistance to government with policy, programme and project design;
— helping NGOs to strengthen their outreach to working children;
— working directly with employers' and workers' organizations;
— providing non-formal education for working children.

We can distinguish two types of approach to helping working children.

Direct support (DS) is one type of intervention and means that the project works directly with children and their families through the provision of services such as education and training, health care, protected work, and so on, or by means of direct support to governments through, for example, technical assistance in drafting a policy document. Many projects, though, concern themselves with the second type of intervention called *institutional development (ID)*, i.e. strengthening NGO or governmental organizations to deliver better services to children and their families. These are the *direct recipients* of the project, and the intention is to improve their capability so that *at a later stage* they can deliver better or more services to the target group. So most ID projects have a training component. With ID projects it is very important to distinguish between what the project staff will do and what the institution will be capable of doing — training staff who leave or who do not pass on their skills, or having experts take over and run an organization rather than develop its staff, leaves institutions worse off and is therefore self-defeating. Projects can therefore be defined as either DS or ID, or a combination of the two.

Institutional development projects have a multiplier effect, i.e. more people will be reached. The multiplier effect can be very considerable from, for example, training a group of 50 labour in-spectors in child labour regulation, or through a "training the trainers" project. Often projects will combine both approaches. For example, a project might work initially with a group of, say, 500 child workers providing them with a comprehensive range of services in the short term (i.e. direct support). Then it might move on to improve the capability of community-based NGOs to deliver more adequate services, or of government, through the development of Child Labour Units, to initiate and coordinate policies, programmes and projects (i.e. institutional development).

Finally, whatever approach is adapted by the project, the effective use of communication is an important feature of all attempts to assist working children (Box Five).

Box Five

COMMUNICATION STRATEGIES IN PROJECT DESIGN

It must never be forgotten that it is people who bring about development. There can be no change for the better without the informed participation of people, without mobilizing their capacities and energies, and without increasing their knowledge and skills. Effective communication is, therefore, one of the key conditions for project success. Remember also that child labour remains a problem largely because it is invisible. The most exploited and endangered children largely go unnoticed. The first and most important step towards protecting them is to bring their situation out into the open, and to the attention of the government, campaigning groups and the general public. Communication strategies therefore need to be planned at the project design stage.

CHAPTER SUMMARY

Project design begins with identifying:

A problem
What is the nature of the child labour problem which justifies the project?

The project strategy
What do you want to do, for whom, with whom and how? Is the best approach direct support and/or institutional development?

The target group
Who are the intended beneficiaries?

The partners
Whom will the project work with and through, i.e. what is the institutional framework?

4. Key elements in project design 2: From objectives to inputs

4.1. Introduction

After the description of the strategy, target groups and partners, projects always contain the following four elements:

— objectives;

— outputs;

— activities;

— inputs.

These elements are interrelated, and if the linkages between them are clear enough this will enable the project designer to predict that:

— if the inputs are available, then the activities take place;

— if the activities take place, then the outputs will be produced;

— if the outputs are produced, then the objective(s) will be achieved.

Not only is it important to ensure these linkages between components, but it is also vital to ensure that each is in proportion (figure 2). For example, avoid overambitious objectives which do not match available inputs.

Figure 2.   *Linkages between project elements*

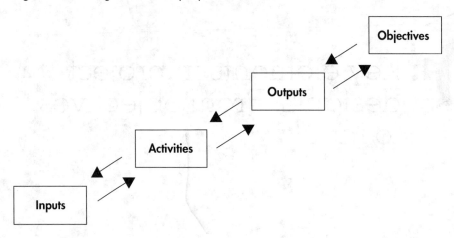

Make sure that the various key elements of the project are coherent and are clearly linked together, i.e. if the *inputs* are provided, the planned *activities* carried out and the *outputs* produced, is it likely that the stated *objective* (s) will be achieved?

4.2. Objectives

An objective is a simple expression of a desired end and can usually be arrived at by turning the problem on its head (or inverting it), as in the example below:

> EXAMPLE:
> *Direct support project*
> *Problem:* There are 1,000 child workers under the age of 12 currently working in factories in the carpet-weaving industry in the district of Atlantis.
> *Inversion into an immediate objective:* 1,000 child workers under the age of 12 currently working in factories in the carpet-weaving industry in the district of Atlantis will be removed from work and absorbed into full-time education.

In project documents one usually finds different types of objectives, or aims of the project. One typically finds long-term and short-term objectives. Long-term objectives are called *development objectives* and short-term objectives are called *immediate objectives.*

The development objective

The development objective is the ultimate aim of a project — why is it being undertaken? There is usually only one development objective in child labour projects. *This is the elimination of child labour and, pending this, the protection of working children.* But this is a long-term goal, and will by definition be beyond any one project's scope and time-scale. The keyword *"contribute to"* best describes the development objective: while progress towards this aim may be observed, it will be difficult to attribute it clearly to a single project. This alone signifies a need for projects to fit into policies and programmes, and further to link development objectives to the development priorities of the government of the country and of NGOs.

The immediate objective

The immediate objective is the situation that is expected to be present at the end of the project. As a general rule immediate objectives should be kept to a minimum (between one and three). The keyword here is *"to achieve"*. In formulating the immediate objective the designer should precisely name who will benefit directly from the project and state the effect which is sought by the end of the project (Box Six gives advice on writing immediate objectives). It is helpful to identify the approach of the project: Is it an institutional development project (ID), a direct support project (DS) or a combination of both? It is also important to be realistic. *Poor formulation of immediate objectives is the single greatest cause of poor project design and therefore of project failure.* Here are some examples of formulated immediate objectives:

Box Six

WRITING IMMEDIATE OBJECTIVES

Words, words, words . . . In writing immediate objectives there are certain words and phrases which may mean different things to different people. Make sure that you understand what you mean by these and that they are fully explained. Try to be as concrete as possible. Here are some examples:

child slaves	effective
street children	empowered
disadvantaged groups	comprehensive
integrated	appropriate
coordinated	viable
raised quality	awareness
enhanced	consciousness
increased	action-oriented
reinforced	pilot project
strengthened	popular participation of children
expanded	child-centred
improved	grass roots
self-reliant	

EXAMPLES:

Direct support project:

At the end of the project 300 children under 14 years in the district of Atlantis will have been removed from the mining industry and absorbed into an experimental non-formal education programme.

Institutional development project:

At the end of the project the Ministry of Labour will have established a child labour unit capable of formulating and coordinating government child labour policies, planning and programmes.

4.3. Outputs

*O*utputs are the products which result from the project activities. The keyword is *"to produce"*. Examples might be materials, curricula, reports, draft policies produced or people trained. Some outputs may need to be produced well before the end of the project; if so, give the scheduled completion date. Sometimes it is difficult to make a distinction between objectives and outputs. As the saying goes: *"You can lead a horse to water, but you cannot make it drink"*. Getting the horse to the water trough is the output, that it then drinks is an objective. Of course, if you have done a thorough problem analysis, you should be able to demonstrate that the horse wanted a drink in the first place.

In a typical ID project outputs take the form of staff trained, reports produced or materials produced, as in the example below:

EXAMPLE:

Objective:

To have strengthened the capability of the Ministry of Labour in enforcing legislation on child labour in the carpet industries.

Outputs:

By the end of the project 50 labour inspectors will have been trained in child labour regulations within the carpet industries.

A manual for labour inspectors on child labour will have been produced.

Reports will have been produced on working conditions in factories using child labour in the carpet industries in the district of Atlantis.

4.4. Activities

*A*ctivities are the actions undertaken to produce the desired outputs, i.e. what will be done, not the results themselves. The keyword is *"to do"*. Producing one output usually requires that you undertake a number of activities. It is important not to confuse activities with outputs, though they may look similar. In the case of ID projects, activities are undertaken for and with the direct recipients. In DS projects, activities are undertaken for and with the target group.

EXAMPLE:

To produce the outputs set out in the above example the project will need to undertake a number of activities. It will:

— organise five workshops for labour inspectors;

— develop training materials and field-test these in workshops;

— commission a consultant, based at the local university, to investigate child labour in the unregulated sector of the garment, fireworks and tapestry industries.

A good way to set out your activities is through a work-plan. You can start drafting one in the project document (see figure 3). The project team will certainly need a more detailed one later on to ensure that activities take place in an optimum way during project implementation. In fact, the timing aspect is a good way of distinguishing outputs from activities: outputs are produced by a certain date, while activities describe the project process and therefore take place over a certain period.

Figure 3. *Project work-plan*

It may be useful to present the timing of the activities in the form of a bar chart:

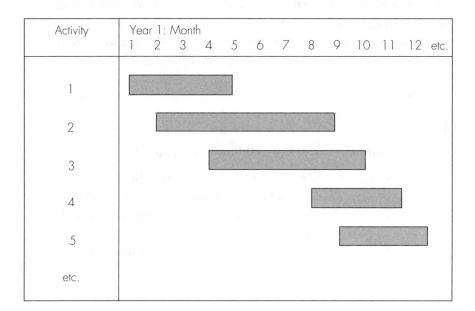

4.5. Inputs

*I*nputs *are the funds, equipment, expertise, human resources, and so on, necessary for carrying out the activities.* There is a continuing need for realism, as the project designer must decide what are the minimum resources needed to carry out the project and who will provide them. Realism is also necessary in relation to partners and their capability. For example, there is little point in overloading an over-stretched Ministry of Labour by asking for hundreds of inspections from a handful of inspectors.

Inputs must be named at all levels — international, national and NGO. If the projects' results are to be sustainable, inputs need to come from the local and national level. Inputs from the recipient country do not always need to be described in money terms; they can also be in kind. If you prepare a document, make sure you always list the inputs that your organization can provide in terms of staff, and so on, and be clear about what you want from outside agencies. Do not ask for a lump sum to be spent for unclear purposes. Ask for concrete inputs.

EXAMPLE:

Bad input: $5,000 is required for equipment.

Good inputs: $2,000 for a photocopier capable of running 300 copies per week; $3,000 for computer facilities, i.e. one desktop personal computer, one printer, word processing/database/desktop publishing software programmes (3).

4.6. Indicators, assumptions and preconditions

Other important project component elements are: indicators; assumptions; and preconditions.

Indicators

Indicators are precise, often measurable factors, which help both to explain the stated objectives and allow for project evaluation because they provide evidence as to whether outputs have led to the achievement of objectives. The project designer must be able to identify what evidence will be used to find out how successful the project has been. Objectives are rarely stated in precise terms as, for example, "reduction of child workers in X hazardous occupations by Y per cent". More often, they are formulated using expressions like "strengthened", "enhanced" or "expanded". A word like "enhanced" will mean different things to different people (see Box Six). To explain what you mean, particularly to a potential financing agency, precision needs to be added to the immediate objective, and you need to set out the criteria by which the success of the project will be judged. This is done by means of indicators. Of course, if your objectives are precisely defined in measurable or clearly verifiable terms, then it may be less important to state indicators.

In formulating indicators, it is again useful to distinguish projects by their approach: ID and DS. In DS projects, indicators will reveal the extent to which the target group is better off as a result of the project. In the case of an ID project, indicators of the achievement of the immediate objective will usually refer to what the institution is capable of doing at the end of the project. In order to reflect the different aspects of an immediate objective, several indicators will usually be needed.

As with so much else in project design, it is important to be realistic. In the first instance, try to avoid an objective which is overambitious, given your resources, capability or time-scale.

Gathering evidence is critical to demonstrating your case. Most of this evidence should be quantifiable, whilst other indicators may lend themselves to a simple YES/NO verification. It follows from this that it makes little sense to give indicators for which you can provide no baseline data and/or no corresponding information at the end of the project. Indicators should be practical and cheap, and should reflect changes directly attributable to the project.

There are dangers in providing examples of indicators in isolation from immediate objectives, because what might look like an indicator for one project could appear more like an output for another. Nevertheless, below are examples of possible indicators placed in the context of immediate objectives and likely outputs:

EXAMPLES:

Direct support project

Immediate objective:

At the end of the project 200 migrant children will be removed from the plantation sector and absorbed into an experimental child development centre.

Outputs:

— 200 places provided for migrant children in non-formal education.

— 200 migrant children provided with vocational skill training.

— 200 migrant children provided with nutrition and health services.

Indicators:

— the educational attainment of 200 migrant children was X and is now Y.

— the health status of 200 migrant children was X and is now Y.

— vocational skill levels of 200 migrant children was X and is now Y.

Institutional development project

Immediate objective:

At the end of the project the Ministry of Labour will have established a child labour unit capable of formulating and coordinating government child labour policies, planning and programmes.

Indicator:

Does it function? YES/NO.

Assumptions

Throughout the life of a project, external factors beyond the control of the project management play a key role. They can be economic, social, political or environmental. Examples could include the assumptions that trained staff remain within their specialism, or that there is continued government commitment to the project. These external factors are called risks or assumptions. A well-designed project, under normal circumstances, should be expected to attain its objectives successfully.

The aim of good project design is in part to progressively minimize assumptions, from project idea to completed document.

These risk factors may operate at all levels in the design process. Here again the designer should be realistic. Try to explain why there is good reason to expect certain external factors or assumptions to materialize. If you have followed the logical framework approach, consulted the target beneficiaries, incorporated lessons learned from project evaluation and carried out a good problem analysis, you may not need to name too many assumptions by the end of the project document. Perhaps one or two will be left. Stating assumptions would appear at first glance to weaken project design and make the project less attractive to financing agencies. However, financing agencies are less likely to have confidence in project documents which present too optimistic a picture. Inclusion of these risk factors makes the project more realistic, and therefore the design is in fact strengthened.

As far as possible, try to state what will happen if certain assumptions do not materialize: "If this happens, we will do the following. . .". This is called contingency planning.

Preconditions

There are other elements which might appear like assumptions but are really factors necessary *before* a project can go ahead. First, there is the interest of the target beneficiaries, which needs to be established in advance. Second, key inputs and organizational arrangements have to be available. These we call *preconditions,* but other terms used are prerequisites and prior obligations. They might include the cooperation of the government, and the use of its machinery to reach and deliver services to working children, or the setting up of coordinating mechanisms such as a project advisory committee.

---

*You cannot **assume** the interest of the target group; you must **know** it in advance. You cannot **assume** that organizations will cooperate and contribute to your project; you must **ensure** this in advance.*

: :

<table>
<tr><td colspan="2" align="center">CHAPTER SUMMARY</td></tr>
<tr><td>***Project element***</td><td>***Keywords***</td></tr>
<tr><td>*Development objective*</td><td>"The long-term *aim* of the project is to have *contributed* to . . ."</td></tr>
<tr><td>*Immediate objective*</td><td>"The project will establish the capacity to *achieve* . . ."</td></tr>
<tr><td>*Outputs*</td><td>"To *produce* . . . by a certain date."</td></tr>
<tr><td>*Activities*</td><td>"To *do* . . . during a certain period."</td></tr>
<tr><td>*Inputs*</td><td>"We *require* . . . to undertake the following activities . . ."</td></tr>
<tr><td>*Indicators*</td><td>"Prior to the project the situation *was* . . . and *is* now. . ."</td></tr>
<tr><td>*Assumptions*</td><td>" The *risk factors* at this stage of the project are . . ."" In case . . . happens, the project will do . . . "</td></tr>
<tr><td>*Preconditions*</td><td>"The project *cannot start without* . . . from . . . "</td></tr>
</table>

: :

5. Key elements in project design 3: Monitoring and evaluation

5.1. Introduction

Monitoring and evaluation are the final elements of the project cycle. It is important to think right at the beginning about how and when the project will provide reports on progress, and how it will be evaluated. In good project design it is essential to state the reporting, monitoring and evaluation procedures. For example:

— When will progress reports be prepared (e.g. every six or 12 months)?

— When will the project be evaluated (e.g. part way through; at the end; some time after the end of the project)?

— How will the project be evaluated (e.g. using internal and/or external people)?

— Who will take part in the evaluation (e.g. project staff, beneficiaries, external funding agencies)?

5.2. Monitoring

Monitoring is concerned largely with ensuring that inputs lead to outputs. It is essential for the project management to make regular progress reports on project implementation — that inputs are being made available as planned, that activities are taking place in line with the work-plan and that outputs are being produced on schedule. It is also important to know what changes, if any, have taken place, and for what reasons. Project management must always be in a position to adapt the project to new needs and conditions which could not have been foreseen at the project design stage.

5.3. What is evaluation?

*E*valuation is the act of discovering whether we are achieving, or are likely to achieve, our objectives.* It must be distinguished both from *project appraisal,* which is an assessment *prior to* deciding whether to undertake a project, and *monitoring,* which is the continuous overview of the implementation of a project, involving the regular *reporting* of basic information. Evaluation is an essential activity which feeds back into current project execution and future project design (Box Seven). Evaluation is thus a key tool for:

— improving the management of ongoing projects;

— improving the preparation of new projects; and

— providing inputs into broader programme evaluation.

Project documents are explanatory tools and they must provide clues for evaluators to assess the *relative* success or failure of projects. Evaluation is concerned with a range of issues dealing with effects and impact:

Effectiveness:	To what extent has the project achieved, or is it likely to achieve, its objectives?
Efficiency:	Do the expected project results continue to justify the cost?
Relevance:	Does the project continue to make sense — are its objectives relevant to the problem?

Validity of design:	Is the design logical and coherent, and are the linkages between components clear?
Unanticipated effects:	Is the project having any significant effects, either negative or positive?
Alternative strategies:	Is there, or would there have been, a more effective or efficient way to approach the problem?
Causality:	What factors affected project performance?
Sustainability:	What is the likelihood that project benefits will be sustained after the withdrawal of external support?

5.4. Types of evaluation

There are two ways of categorizing evaluation. First, evaluation can be defined in terms of *timing* — at which point does it take place? Second, it can be defined in terms of *personnel* —is it an internal or external exercise?

Timing

— *Interim evaluation* looks at project outputs, likely effects and impact *while the project is being implemented*; it provides project managers with the data required to assess, and if necessary adjust, policies, objectives, institutional arrangements and resources. It is a taking stock — an assessment at one point in time.

— *Terminal evaluation* is the analysis *at the end of a project*, or a phase of a project; it provides decision-makers with information for future planning and project design.

— Ex-post *evaluation* refers to an assessment of a project *some time after its completion*, perhaps two to three years later. This might be necessary to find out, for example, the long-term impact on aspects of child development or the sustainability of project benefits.

BOX SEVEN

WHY IS EVALUATION IMPORTANT?

The cost of not evaluating is extremely high. First of all, a lack of facts about results reduces the ability to learn from experience with working children, and this hinders progress.

Second, in the absence of information about results many decisions are based on inappropriate criteria. Factors that should be of secondary importance — such as ideology, interpersonal relationships (often a major cause of project failure) or bureaucratic convenience — end up as the bases of decisions that should have been arrived at according to what produces the best results. Finally, project credibility can suffer when expenditures of human and material resources cannot be linked to positive changes for children, families or communities. By definition, projects that know little about their results cannot be well managed, and neither national governments nor financing agencies can be expected to invest substantial resources on activities whose impact cannot be ascertained. For example, it is sometimes observed that the community-based model of services for working children has not yet been successfully taken up to a larger scale. For that to happen, considerable public sector investment would in most cases be required. Yet, without concrete evidence that such community services yield long-term positive results in the lives of working children, how would a government properly justify investing substantial public resources during a time of stringent budget constraints?

Personnel

— *Internal evaluation* is conducted by the project staff, in cooperation with partners and beneficiaries, often as a form of ongoing self-evaluation.

— *External evaluation* uses outsiders whose distance from the project can lend greater objectivity.

5.5. Some pitfalls to avoid

Most organizations serving working children have always somehow assessed their progress and effectiveness, even if only informally and as part of their ongoing operations. Mostly they have compared their progress with their intentions. This approach, which often tends to focus on project output rather than impact (e.g. counting how many lunches were served instead of monitoring the nutritional status of the children eating them), is frequently used for reports to financing agencies. However, it may provide only limited insight into whether a project is achieving its aims.

5.6. Approaches to evaluation

Evaluation styles vary. The evaluator could take on the role of a technician who measures a variable identified by the client, e.g. child workers' use of services. Taking a different approach, the evaluator could simply describe the pattern of strengths and weaknesses of a particular project in relation to certain stated objectives, e.g. working street children find it difficult to combine formal education with their work commitments. The popular view of an evaluator is of a judge who determines whether the project has met its objectives.

Finally, evaluation could be more concerned with the present — with the current concerns and perceptions held by the project stakeholders. Here the evaluator would attempt to get at the meaning people attach to events rather than attempt to arrive at "the truth" about the past. For example, the evaluator might be presented with the fact that 100 labour inspectors had been trained. He or she might wish to go beyond this fact to determine whether the training addressed the needs of trainees and whether they were using their new knowledge and skills. Is 100 trained good or bad? Could it, or should it, have been more? Did the training achieve results? Would different training have been better? How? Is training the best solution to the problem? And so on.

Effective evaluation is likely to combine all, or a number of, these styles. But, in addition, what is vital is *the process* of involving all those who have a stake in the project, especially the target beneficiaries and the partners. An emphasis on team evaluation using "external" and "internal" people, conducted as an educational process, has one other important consequence — it brings people together in a *shared owner- ship* of the project, and a commitment to act on the recommendations of the evaluation.

CHAPTER SUMMARY

Question	*Answer*
What is monitoring?	Monitoring essentially concentrates on ensuring that inputs lead to outputs; it is undertaken by project management.
What is evaluation?	Evaluation is concerned with assessing the extent to which a project has met or is likely to meet its objectives, i.e. with effect and impact.
Why is evaluation important?	Good evaluation is essential for progress because it provides lessons about what works (and where) and what does not (and why). It is important to build these lessons into current and future project design.
How should evaluation be conducted?	As a learning exercise involving all those people, both internal and external, who have a stake in the project.

PART III

PRACTICAL TOOLS

6. International labour standards

P art III starts with an examination of international labour standards (ILS) because they are a major tool for project designers. Projects must wherever possible not only conform to the relevant ILS, but should contain practical measures to promote them, e.g. through public awareness campaigns. In this chapter we provide you with a summary of the most important Convention and Recommendation on child labour. Chapter 10 provides guidance on how they might be incorporated into a project document.

A major part of the ILO's work on child labour has been the adoption by the International Labour Conference of a series of Conventions and Recommendations dealing with the employment or work of children and young persons. *Conventions are subject to ratification and create binding obligations on States who ratify them, while Recommendations complement Conventions and are intended to serve as guidelines for national policy.* The first Convention dealing with child labour was adopted at the first session of the International Labour Conference in 1919. This instrument — the Minimum Age (Industry) Convention, 1919 (No. 5) — fixed at 14 years the minimum age for admission of children to industrial employment. Subsequently, many international labour Conventions and Recommendations were adopted prohibiting the employment of children under a certain age and regulating their conditions of work in particular sectors or occupations.

National legislation on child labour has been strongly influenced by international labour standards. The approach adopted in Conventions has been to set a minimum age for admission to employment or work, either for a given sector of the economy or for the whole of it, and to allow certain exceptions where circumstances warrant this. The Conventions adopted before 1973 set minimum ages for employment or work in industry, non-industrial employment, agriculture and underground work, and at sea. This sectoral approach allowed countries to ratify Conventions which applied to their own particular circumstances. Many countries were not — and still are not — capable of setting and implementing a minimum age for employment or work in all sectors of the economy. By ratifying and implementing a Convention which applies only to a limited sector, these countries were able to make progress.

In 1973 the Conference decided to establish a general instrument on the subject, which would gradually replace those applicable to limited economic sectors. It therefore adopted *the Minimum Age Convention (No. 138) and Recommendation (No. 146) in 1973.* These instruments are general in scope, and in principle cover all economic sectors and all employment or work, whether or not it is performed under a contract of employment. However, Convention No. 138 is not a static instrument, and is aimed at encouraging the progressive improvement of standards and at promoting sustained action to attain its objectives. The obligations assumed by ratifying States are flexible, and conditioned by national circumstances and the level of the standards already achieved in each country. Provision is therefore made for several kinds of exclusions or exceptions in coverage, scope and standards.

Minimum ages set out in Convention No. 138

	General	Exceptions
Basic minimum age	15	14
Hazardous work	18	16
Light work	13 to 15	12 to 14

Box Eight

MINIMUM AGE CONVENTION, 1973 (No. 138)

Article 1

Each Member for which this Convention is in force undertakes to pursue a national policy designed to ensure the effective abolition of child labour and to raise progressively the minimum age for admission to employment or work to a level consistent with the fullest physical and mental development of young persons.

Article 2

1. Each Member which ratifies this Convention shall specify, in a declaration appended to its ratification, a minimum age for admission to employment or work within its territory and on means of transport registered in its territory. . .

   . . .

3. The minimum age specified in pursuance of paragraph 1 of this Article shall not be less than the age of completion of compulsory schooling and, in any case, shall not be less than 15 years.

4. Notwithstanding the provisions of paragraph 3 of this Article, a Member whose economy and educational facilities are insufficiently developed may, after consultation with the organizations of employers and workers concerned, where such exist, initially specify a minimum age of 14 years.

   . . .

Article 3

1. The minimum age for admission to any type of employment or work which by its nature or the circumstances in which it is carried out is likely to jeopardize the health, safety or morals of young persons shall not be less than 18 years.

   . . .

3. Notwithstanding the provisions of paragraph 1 of this Article, national laws or regulations or the competent authority may, after consultation with the organizations of employers and

workers concerned, where such exist, authorize employment or work as from the age of 16 years on condition that the health, safety and morals of the young persons concerned are fully protected and that the young persons have received adequate specific instruction or vocational training in the relevant branch of activity.

. . .

Article 7

1. National laws or regulations may permit the employment or work of persons 13 to 15 years of age on light work which is —
(a) not likely to be harmful to their health or development; and
(b) not such as to prejudice their attendance at school, their participation in vocational orientation or training programmes approved by the competent authority or their capacity to benefit from the instruction received.

2. National laws or regulations may also permit the employment or work of persons who are at least 15 years of age but have not yet completed their compulsory schooling on work which meets the requirements set forth in sub-paragraphs (a) and (b) of paragraph 1 of this Article.

. . .

4. Notwithstanding the provisions of paragraphs 1 and 2 of this Article, a Member which has availed itself of the provisions of paragraph 4 of Article 2 may, for as long as it continues to do so, substitute the ages 12 and 14 for the ages 13 and 15 in paragraph 1 and the age 14 for the age 15 in paragraph 2 of this Article.

. . .

Article 9

1. All necessary measures, including the provision of appropriate penalties, shall be taken by the competent authority to ensure the effective enforcement of the provisions of this Convention.

. . .

3. National laws or regulations or the competent authority shall prescribe the registers or other documents which shall be kept and made available by the employer; such registers or documents shall contain the names and ages or dates of birth, duly certified wherever possible, of persons whom he employs or who work for him and who are less than 18 years of age.

. . .

Box NINE

RATIFICATIONS OF THE MINIMUM AGE CONVENTION, 1973 (No. 138), AS OF 1992

State	Minimum age specified	State	Minimum age specified
Algeria	16	Luxembourg	15
Antigua and Barbuda	16	Malta	16
Belarus	16	Mauritius	15
Belgium	15	Netherlands	15
Bulgaria	16	Nicaragua	14
Costa Rica	15	Niger	14
Cuba	15	Norway	15
Dominica	15	Poland	15
Equatorial Guinea	14	Romania	16
France	16	Russian Federation	16
Germany	15	Rwanda	14
Greece	15	Spain	15
Guatemala	14	Sweden	15
Honduras	14	Togo	14
Iraq	15	Ukraine	16
Ireland	15	Uruguay	15
Israel	15	Venezuela	14
Italy	15	Yugoslavia	15
Kenya	16	Zambia	15
Libyan Arab Jamahiriya	15		

The Minimum Age Recommendation, No. 146 (1973), provides a framework for policy development. It covers the issues of national policy, minimum age, hazardous employment or work, conditions of employment, and enforcement.

Child labour policy is placed to begin with in the broadest possible context of the need to pursue anti-poverty and full employment strategies, combined with the progressive extension of social welfare and educational provisions. The Recommendation stresses the need for consistency between minimum age requirements for employment or work and the end of compulsory schooling or vocational training. It further suggests the need to set 16 years as the minimum age objective for employment and 18 years for hazardous work.

Recommendation No. 146 necessarily emphasizes enforcement and regulation, citing the need to strengthen the labour inspectorate through training and to ensure a system of registration for births and of young workers.

Box Ten

MINIMUM AGE RECOMMENDATION, 1973 (No. 146)

I. National Policy

1. To ensure the success of the national policy provided for in Article 1 of the Minimum Age Convention, 1973, high priority should be given to planning for and meeting the needs of children and youth in national development policies and programmes and to the progressive extension of the inter-related measures necessary to provide the best possible conditions of physical and mental growth for children and young persons.

. . .

4. Full-time attendance at school or participation in approved vocational orientation or training programmes should be required and effectively ensured up to an age at least equal to that specified for admission to employment in accordance with Article 2 of the Minimum Age Convention, 1973.

...

II. Minimum Age

6. The minimum age should be fixed at the same level for all sectors of economic activity.

7. (1) Members should take as their objective the progressive raising to 16 years of the minimum age for admission to employment or work specified in pursuance of Article 2 of the Minimum Age Convention, 1973.

(2) Where the minimum age for employment or work covered by Article 2 of the Minimum Age Convention, 1973, is still below 15 years, urgent steps should be taken to raise it to that level.

8. Where it is not immediately feasible to fix a minimum age for all employment in agriculture and in related activities in rural areas, a minimum age should be fixed at least for employment on plantations and in the other agricultural undertakings referred to in Article 5, paragraph 3, of the Minimum Age Convention, 1973.

III. Hazardous Employment or Work

9. Where the minimum age for admission to types of employment or work which are likely to jeopardize the health, safety or morals of young persons is still below 18 years, immediate steps should be taken to raise it to that level.

10. (1) In determining the types of employment or work to which Article 3 of the Minimum Age Convention, 1973, applies, full account should be taken of relevant international labour standards, such as those concerning dangerous substances, agents or processes (including ionizing radiations), the lifting of heavy weights and underground work.

. . .

V. Enforcement

14. (1) Measures to ensure the effective application of the Minimum Age Convention, 1973, and of this Recommendation should include —

(a) the strengthening as necessary of labour inspection and related services, for instance by the special training of inspectors to detect abuses in the employment or work of children and young persons and to correct such abuses; and

(b) the strengthening of services for the improvement and inspection of training in undertakings.

(2) Emphasis should be placed on the role which can be played by inspectors in supplying information and advice on effective means of complying with relevant provisions as well as in securing their enforcement.

(3) Labour inspection and inspection of training in undertakings should be closely coordinated to provide the greatest economic efficiency and, generally, the labour administration services should work in close cooperation with the services responsible for the education, training, welfare and guidance of children and young persons.

15. Special attention should be paid —

(a) to the enforcement of provisions concerning employment in hazardous types of employment or work; . . .

16. The following measures should be taken to facilitate the verification of ages:

(a) the public authorities should maintain an effective system of birth registration, which should include the issue of birth certificates;

(b) employers should be required to keep and to make available to the competent authority registers or other documents indicating the names and ages or dates of birth, duly certified wherever possible, not only of children and young persons employed by them but also of those receiving vocational orientation or training in their undertakings;

(c) children and young persons working in the streets, in outside stalls, in public places, in itinerant occupations or in other circumstances which make the checking of employers' records impracticable should be issued licences or other documents indicating their eligibility for such work.

7. Finding out about child labour

7.1. Introduction

T his chapter gives an overview of where to find information on child workers, in terms of written materials, people and organizations, and how to go about collecting it. Improving the capacity to collect baseline information is, as we saw in Chapter 3, an important priority. Project design needs to begin with a sound problem or situation analysis, as projects should be based on a foundation of fact rather than myth, prejudice or ignorance.

7.2. What is problem analysis?

P *roblem analysis* identifies the needs and characteristics of a target group and stimulates new forms of response. It typically incorporates at least three elements.

The definition and description of a situation or problem

This entails identifying the overall dimensions and features of the child labour problem, in order to understand:

— *the nature of the problem.* What is the exact problem or situation which the children face? How does this situation affect them? What are their main needs? What are the factors behind the problem?

— *the extent of the child labour problem and distribution of those affected.* How many children are in this situation and what is their geographic distribution? What is their age, sex, class and ethnic distribution?

— *the family and social context.* What are the children's cultural, social and economic characteristics? What is their family, community and institutional setting?

— *the wider socio-economic context* that gives rise to the problem, e.g. problems of urbanization and a growing population of street children; growing poverty due to problems of structural adjustment and external debt, etc.

Analysis of existing responses to the problem

Part of the function of problem analysis is to assess existing welfare and development measures that have an impact on the lives of the target group. This involves looking at:

— *legislative and policy responses.* What laws (e.g. minimum age legislation) and policies affect these children and in what ways? How effective are they? Which measures have worked and which have not? Why?

— *programme and project responses.* What programmes and projects exist to address these problems and what approaches do they employ? How effective and efficient are they and what is their coverage? What has worked and what has not? Why?

— *the various actors.* Which government agencies and/or NGOs are active in combating child labour? What do they do? Are they effective or not? What is their capacity?

Assessment of unmet needs

The aim of assessing existing responses to the children's various needs is in part to identify the most effective approaches and also to highlight possible failures and problems of present provision for working children. This involves looking at:

— *gaps between problems and responses.* What are the discrepancies (in terms of both relevance and scope) between the problem and the responses addressing it? Which of these gaps are most important?

— *what is needed to reduce these discrepancies.* What types of action would be most effective? What should be the criteria of success? What are alternative points of intervention? What is already being done which is useful, and what else should be done?

— *the changes over time.* What are the trends in the children's condition? How have the responses to their situation changed? Are the responses becoming more or less effective in addressing the children's problems?

7.3. How to conduct problem analysis: Who should be involved?

T he most effective way to conduct problem analysis — at national or local level — is through a partnership. This helps bring diverse resources and experiences together. Reaching children at risk demands team vision, spirit and collaboration, involving all interested parties, both public and private.

At the national level, problem analysis should be a multi-agency endeavour involving centrally the Ministry of Labour allied to the Ministries of Education, Health and Welfare and other relevant social ministries, and NGOs. Local-level problem analysis may be undertaken by voluntary organizations, municipal authorities, academic institutions and religious groups. It is always important to incorporate the views of working children and their families as far as is possible and practicable.

7.4. Possible sources of information

The challenge in information gathering in child labour is to find cost-effective methods. The techniques should neither be too quick and superficial nor too long and expensive, particularly for small organizations. *The system of key informants (Box Eleven) is of particular value.*

BOX ELEVEN

KEY INFORMANTS

One way to understand the total system of child work in a community is to construct a chain of key informants. The key informant is a person who is accessible, willing to talk, and has great depth of knowledge about an area and its activities. In any community it should not take too long to construct such a chain (ministry officials, labour inspectors, schoolteachers, religious leaders, community leaders, employers, trade union officials, health and welfare officers, police, children, etc.). Each link in the chain may see the child labour problem differently. And though you must be aware of this, and not necessarily believe everything key informants say, a skilled interviewer can extract not just qualitative information, but possibly an enormous amount of quantitative data concerning the incidence of child labour in the area.

Secondary material

Before undertaking any new research, it is worth finding out what material on the subject already exists, as there is no point in reinventing the wheel. There are two types of secondary material, both of which can usefully be consulted when you undertake a problem analysis.

Official documents produced by national and local government can provide vital information on legislation, public policy, the structure of statutory agencies, and professional practice and programmes in the public sector. Statutory bodies also sometimes undertake sectoral studies that can be of great use and interest. For example, labour ministries in many countries undertake regular household surveys on labour force participation. Official documents may include censuses, surveys, policy statements, professional guidelines, minutes of meetings, registers, published legislative acts and court proceedings, among others. But perhaps the key resource is to be found in education statistics, and in particular the figures for school enrolment (and drop-out rates), as most children not at school can be presumed to be working. It is necessary to be careful, however, as even this data may underestimate the extent of child labour because the majority of children in urban areas both go to school and work. Indeed they may work in order to go to school.

Be aware too that official survey data are often based on restrictive definitions. For example, official statistics on the economically active population often exclude youngsters who work part time or in the informal sector. The same is true of unpaid children, such as the ones who accompany their parents in agricultural labour, or who work as domestics in exchange for their keep. This seriously undercounts working children, and often those in hazardous occupations deserving priority concern.

Unofficial documents consist of the mass of information produced by private individuals and the media, academic institutions, non-governmental agencies, the church and other bodies. These materials range from unpublished theses, evaluations, surveys and reports to published books, television and radio programmes and newspaper articles. These sources may provide good information. However, such sources sometimes present an over-sensational treatment which can distort the picture of child labour.

Children

It may seem unnecessary to state that children are an important source of information. Yet a remarkable number of studies of working children are based solely on information obtained from adults. In most cases children are not even informed that they are the subjects of investigation. Since ultimately the aim of the problem analysis is to develop effective policy and programming to change their lives, then clearly children's feelings and views, their beliefs and aspirations, are crucially relevant to the investigation. Try to identify what they see as a problem and what they would like to change.

Institutions, professional bodies and welfare practitioners

There are a variety of institutions, professional groups and individuals in all countries that work with children in one capacity or another. These institutions could be statutory or private and might include schools, hospitals, community health centres, the courts, orphanages, lodgings, night shelters, day-care centres and religious centres, among others.

The police, social workers and other professional groups also come into regular contact with children and may be very knowledgeable about their circumstances. In addition, a variety of committed individuals and members of non-governmental organizations, who are specifically concerned and work with children, exist in most countries. Among their number are volunteer street educators, teachers, journalists, auxiliary health workers, lobbyists and others.

Employers' and workers' organizations

Employers are another obvious source of information on working children. Employers' organizations have a responsibility to help regulate child labour and promote awareness of minimum age legislation. Employers who actually employ children should also be contacted. Often it is easier to see and talk with them than with their child workers.

Workers' organizations have an untapped potential in combating child labour. Those trade unions active in organizing marginal workers, and campaigning for the adoption and implementation of ILS, will be an important source of information on working children.

7.5. Methods of investigation

For each source of information there are a number of different methods of obtaining the information. These can be compared for their relative effectiveness and feasibility. It is important to assess which method or methods are most likely to provide the best-quality information, given the time and money available for the investigation.

The techniques used for the collection of data will vary widely according to the kind of information sought, the resources available for the investigation, and the size and problems of the population being studied. For example, intensive methods such as participant observation, which tend to produce qualitative rather than quantitative information, are therefore more suitable for finding out about children's feelings and attitudes. More extensive techniques, such as surveys, can be used for larger populations and for investigations where the information sought is relatively limited and straightforward, and are therefore more suitable for finding out about living conditions, family structures and labour force participation.

Methods for obtaining the information may include:

— observation;

— surveys;

— interviews.

The most effective results can be obtained by using a mix of techniques rather than relying solely on one — this will greatly enrich the findings and render them more reliable. It also allows cross-checking between the various sources of information, and enables the matching of quantitative and qualitative information. Many methods are inexpensive and if used with care and sensitivity can produce extremely good results. But most important of all, the investigation needs to be approached with flexibility, adapting to changes in the target group and in the definition of the problem.

65

Observation

Walking, seeing, talking with people and listening are of fundamental importance to all successful inquiries. Observation is important because there is often a gap between what people might say in a survey and what they do in practice. It is especially suitable then for collecting qualitative information. All problem analysis should begin with direct observation, so that the investigators can gather first impressions without being committed to any particular theme or method of investigation. This might also help to dispel some myths about child labour, as for example, that children are never exploited by their families or that they always work fewer hours than adults. Observation in rural areas has often contradicted such assumptions. There are two approaches to observation:

— *Participant observation* is where the investigator lives and works with the subject group for a long period of time, and discreetly records findings, so as not to disrupt and distort the relationships or activities being studied. Derived from anthropology and sociology, this is rarely used today in the development field.

— *Direct observation* is where the investigator does not live with the subject group for a long period, but may engage in their day-to-day activities. This technique allows for greater flexibility since the investigator can move from one group or location to another. One disadvantage of direct observation is that it takes time and does not easily allow for the collection of quantitative information. And there is always the risk that the group being observed is not representative of the whole.

Box Twelve

THE DANGERS OF "CHILD LABOUR TOURISM"

The phenomenon of "street children", with its loose definitional base, would appear a classic trap for the unwary and superficial observer, driven perhaps by the emotional appeal of the group. Are we talking of all children who earn a living on the street, or those more vulnerable few who have severed all links with their families?

Surveys

This is the technique used most commonly in social investigation. It involves an inquiry into a fixed range of issues among all members, or a sample of members, from a given population. Normally the inquiry is based on a written form, or questionnaire. The number of people covered by a survey is usually much greater than that possible with observation. Therefore, surveys are best applied when quantification is required.

If executed with care and sensitivity, surveys can produce very good information. But they can also be overused. Often the people who design the questionnaires do not take into account the needs and level of skills of those applying them. And sometimes people's expectations of what information can be obtained through a survey are unrealistic.

Inexpensive and small-scale surveys are likely to be more appropriate for local-based organizations. Short questionnaires, using researchers who may be university students, schoolteachers, and so on, can be extremely valuable. This research may also be flexible, using more informal interviewing techniques to gather qualitative insights. A student, for example, who has links with a rural area can be a key informant but also a key researcher, able to find out very quickly and efficiently what needs to be known about child workers in rural areas. Conversely, urban-based, urban-biased students, when used in a rural context, can be worse than useless.

It is important to introduce a warning here. *Surveys depend on the quality of the questionnaire design and of the people who administer them.* A social science background is highly desirable, and it is important to choose interviewers who can establish a rapport with the subject group. Training the interviewers is essential. Your local university social science department could help.

Interviews

In surveys two major kinds of interviewing techniques are used:

— *Structured interviews*. A standard form is used which is designed especially to collect the same information on the people interviewed.

67

In larger surveys the range of possible answers to each question is known. The possible answers may be indicated on the form so that the interviewer may simply mark off the appropriate reply. Structured interviews with predetermined or "closed" answers are particularly suitable for collecting straightforward factual — especially demographic — information. However, it is almost impossible to design a structured interview to produce good answers if the problem being studied is not familiar to the investigators.

— *Unstructured interviews.* This is a more informal approach. There is neither a standard order of questions nor a set way of phrasing them. The interviewer is free to put the questions he or she chooses so long as they follow the themes or broad issues of the investigation. This approach gives the person being interviewed greater control over the direction of the conversation and the information obtained in this way can be extremely varied and rich. Unstructured interviews and surveys based on "open" questions tend to be more effective than structured interviews for learning about attitudes, beliefs, opinions and values. However, it should be remembered that the use of open questions, or unstructured interviews, means that both the collection and analysis of data will take much longer than with structured interviews.

7.6. Rapid appraisal

The ideal approach, particularly for small organizations, is most likely to be a middle course between the extremes of quick appraisal (akin to child labour tourism — see Box Twelve) and large-scale surveys. This has come to be called *rapid appraisal*, i.e. *fairly quick and fairly cost-effective*. Rapid appraisal is not restricted to one methodology, but uses a variety of the methods we have described in this chapter to generate information in a short time. It is a short cut, but need not be a second-rate method. In order to avoid the pitfalls of quick appraisal it is important to follow these principles:

— *Take time.* Many of the defects of quick appraisal stem from haste typified by the brief visit of an outsider.

— *Counter bias.* Think about biases (urban, rural, gender, ethnic, wage-earning, bureaucratic) and deliberately try to counter them. Wherever possible, male bias should be countered by including women in appraisal teams. Thought should also be given to including young people in the team. In some sectors, e.g. plantations, child workers are often members of minority ethnic groups; it may therefore be important to account for this dimension also.

— *Listen and learn.* Assume that poor people and child workers have much valid knowledge that outsiders do not have. Try to see the world as they do. Be open to unexpected information.

— *Multiple approaches.* Investigate the problem using different methods, both to cross-check and to fill out the picture.

CHAPTER SUMMARY

Question	**Answer**
Why is problem analysis important?	Because it provides the foundations for all effective projects and is the starting point for evaluation.
What are the benefits of problem analysis?	You need to understand the situation and the problems facing working children *before* you can hope to design an effective project. Without good information about the situation and the problem, your project may be based on false assumptions, which could make the situation worse, not better.

What do we need to find out?	Which children are in special need — where are they and how many are there? What causes children to be exploited through work?
What are the trends in child labour?	Remember that your project will be conceived in the present, but will have its impact in the future. There is little point in designing a solution to a problem which has become outdated because of trends, for example, in the growth of child labour in the informal sector.
Who should be involved?	There should be a partnership between a variety of public and private organizations at all levels — remember to sample the views of the target group.
Is it difficult to conduct a good problem analysis?	There is little point in pretending that it is easy. Getting information on children can be difficult because researchers tend to concentrate on adults. But, in any case, the cost of not doing it is much too high.
What methods of investigation should be avoided by small-scale organizations?	Methods at opposite ends of the scale — either too quick and superficial or too long and costly.
What is a secondary source?	Written material on the subject, e.g. official documents or research done by others.

Why is observing people important?	It is a way of cross-checking what people say in interviews — what they say and what they do may be quite different.
What are surveys?	They are a method of collecting information using a framework of questions, either structured (using a questionnaire) or unstructured.
What is the difference between a structured and an unstructured interview?	A formal/structured interview uses a questionnaire in which the questions are "closed" (with a limited range of possible responses). In an informal/ unstructured interview the questions are open-ended, allowing a variety of responses from the people interviewed.
Whom should we interview?	Key informants can be useful, but be aware in particular that people in authority may provide rather biased views.
What is rapid appraisal?	It is a middle way between extremes in investigation. Rapid appraisal uses a variety of methods to obtain in-depth information in a relatively short period.

8. How to interview

8.1. Introduction

In the previous chapter we explored the variety of methods that might
be employed in finding out about the nature and extent of child
labour. In this chapter we shall examine interviewing techniques
because the use of interviews is a major way of finding out about child
labour. The chapter concludes with a draft questionnaire.

8.2. Preparing the ground

Before you conduct interviews you need to have identified the
themes or topics which you consider to be central. Out of this
you can build up a list of questions which you might wish to try out or
"pilot" first. Finding good interviewers is in many ways the most crucial
step and is by no means a simple operation in child labour. Intermediaries, often former child workers themselves, can help smooth the way
to establishing a relationship of trust. Remember also to "pilot" your
interviewers. They need careful selection and training. Avoid those who
might intimidate because of their background, status or power.

8.3. Conducting interviews

The interview process can be divided into three stages: *warm-up; interviewing; recording.*

Warm-up

It is never sensible to start with direct questions. The conversation should begin with socially accepted polite talk. Explain the general reasons for the interview. The interviewee must know exactly who the researchers are and the nature of, and reasons for, the survey. You might use this opening period to allow the persons interviewed to talk about a topic they choose, which may complement information obtained in the main interview.

Interviewing

The key to a successful informal interview is to be natural and relaxed while guiding the conversation to a fruitful conclusion. Below are some useful hints on good interviewing techniques:

— Avoid sensitive questions at the beginning.

— Questions that start with *"who, what, where, when, why and how"* always help to establish the situation. Use these as a framework of prompts — they often reveal important information about such things as the division of labour between boys and girls.

— If a question causes silence, or cannot be answered, avoid suggesting answers which reflect the researcher's bias. Ask the question in a different way and possibly later on.

— Use plain, understandable language. Avoid abstract words.

— Keep your own comments, knowledge and conclusions separate from the information obtained directly from the interviewees. Avoid rephrasing a response in your own words, as it is crucial to understand what things mean when referred to in the language of the people themselves.

— Learn how to probe by listening closely, and asking for more details and greater depth, if necessary.

— Questions should always be phrased so that they require explanation rather than a simple YES/NO response, i.e. they should be "open", not "closed".

— Keep questions short; avoid the long and unfocused question.

— Ask one question at a time.

— Avoid "leading questions" which confirm the researcher's own thinking on a topic, e.g. "Do you send your children to work because it will help them to acquire a practical skill necessary for adult life?". Although answers to leading questions are not necessarily wrong, there is no good way of proving this once a leading question has been answered in the affirmative ("yes"). Leading questions make further probing for details much more difficult and subsequent answers less reliable.

— Pay close attention to non-verbal clues. Reading non-verbal reactions can often indicate whether the answers received are truthful.

— Avoid any indication of disbelief, contempt or ridicule of responses given by the interviewees.

— Avoid repeating questions — this may happen in poorly conducted team interviews.

— Beware of the desire in many cultures to please, and therefore for people to provide the answer they think the interviewer wants.

— Place a time limit on the process. If interviewing is done well it is very intensive and tiring; *keep interviews to about one hour at most*. Avoid more than four to five interviews per day.

Recording

Immediately after the interview (or during it, if possible), memory-prompting notes should be made because it is surprising how facts, ideas and important observations that you will "never forget" quickly slip away — perhaps up to 50 per cent of the details of an interview may be lost within 24 hours.

Informal interviews lasting more than 30 minutes will usually be casual enough to allow the writing of some notes during the interview. An official-looking questionnaire should not be used as this may well destroy confidence. How long you should wait before jotting down notes, or writing up full field notes, depends on the setting, the person(s) being interviewed and personal style. If you interview in the morning, for example, you could stop at midday and write up the full notes while they are still fresh in the mind. It is also valuable for the research team to meet daily in the evening to go over notes, review questions and sequencing, and see what patterns may be emerging from the information. It may have struck all interviewers, for example, that almost all girls in domestic work are from the rural areas and are being engaged by "fictional" relatives, i.e. so-called "cousins" or "godparents".

8.4. Group and team interviews

Interviews usually take place on a one-to-one basis. It is also possible to interview a group of people. Alternatively, a number of interviewers may interview an individual person or a group. The latter is called a team interview.

Group interviews have several advantages, including quick access to a larger body of knowledge, and mutual checking. Convening special-ized panels of groups of people, such as employers, might be very revealing of their attitude to child and adult labour, and their awareness of labour legislation and the effects of work on child development. Getting together parents who represent two or three generations could help reveal past, present and expected future attitudes to the economic role of children and the value of education. There is also the benefit of a self-correcting mechanism within the group because if one person puts across an over-favourable picture of his or her own behaviour, others may give a more realistic observation. Group interviews can be difficult when discussing sensitive issues such as child abuse, or where there are social pressures or power relationships in play, which might inhibit an honest response. Here *individual interviews* are more appropriate, and this is the method most likely to be used in the majority of cases.

If you undertake a team interview it is important to make sure that:

— every team member gets to complete his or her questions on a topic before the interview proceeds to another topic;

— no interruptions by other team members occur; and

— every team member takes chronological notes on everything said and a scribe is appointed to write up a draft report.

8.5. Interviewing child workers — Draft questionnaire

It is impossible to produce a standard questionnaire for all contexts in which children may be working. What follows is the *basis* for a general questionnaire to interview working children themselves. Depending on your situation, you should delete or change the questions.

General background data

1. Sex
2. Age
3. Ethnic origin
4. Place of birth

Household composition

1. Number of brothers and sisters and other family or household members
2. Occupation and work activities of parents:
— self-employed
— wage employment
— education of family members

Social relationships

1. Whom do you trust and like most?
2. If you are not living with your parents, what forced you to leave home and why do you not return?
3. What are your relationships with children of your own age?
4. What are your relationships with official figures: welfare officers, police, teachers, priests, etc.?

Personal work histories

1. When did you first work?
2. In what work activities were you involved?
3. Where have you worked and how often have you changed jobs?
4. How were you recruited?
5. Did you change job? If yes, why?
6. How much did you earn in a day?
7. How long did you work?
8. Do you work for yourself or do you have a "boss"?
9. What were your tasks and responsibilities?
10. Who provided you with the capital or tools that you used?
11. What injuries, accidents or health problems have you experienced while at work?
12. Who benefits from any rewards you receive from work?
13. Do you have other (and undisclosed) means of livelihood, e.g. gifts, barters, theft, begging, etc.?
14. How do you use this income?
15. Whom have you worked with — how often have you worked alone?
16. What are the benefits of working?
17. What have you learned from working which you might not have learned any other way?
18. What are the things you most like and dislike about working?

Education

1. Have you attended school — if so, where and what type of school?
2. At what age did you first attend school?
3. How frequent has your attendance been?
4. If you have not attended school, what were the reasons?
5. What grade have you reached?
6. What examinations have you taken and what have been the results?
7. What problems have you encountered at school?
8. What effects has working had on your schooling — have they been combined?
9. How have you combined work and schooling?

The future

1. What aspirations do you have for the future — what do you *hope* to achieve?
2. What expectations do you have for the future — what do you *expect* to achieve?

CHAPTER SUMMARY

Question	Answer
What needs to be done before interviewing takes place?	Start with themes or topics and build up a list of questions from these. Try out the questionnaire first and make sure your interviewers are carefully selected and trained.
How should child workers be approached?	This can be very difficult. You must establish trust and use researchers who can establish a rapport with children. Former child workers can be initial "go-betweens".
What are the "do's" and "don'ts" of interviewing?	There are many. But essentially: *Do* use simple, open questions that are to the point and *do* listen; *don't* ask too many questions at the same time, *don't* ask vague questions, and *don't* put the answer in people's mouth.
Finally, what should you never forget to do after the interview?	To write up your notes. It surprising how quickly the content of an interview is forgotten.

9. The effects of work on children: A checklist

9.1. Introduction

This checklist is a guide to the possible themes or subjects you may wish to choose in conducting problem analysis. Usually it will not be necessary to touch upon all the themes mentioned. Select those which are most useful to what you want to find out.

9.2. How children's work requirements have affected their personal development

In many ways this is the most important theme because it leads to one of the most fundamental questions on child labour: *"What impact does working have on children's lives?"*. Here we would wish to know the effects not only on their immediate health and safety, but also on their long-term physical, intellectual, emotional, social and moral development — of course, work properly structured and integrated into the child's life can be a positive feature. The task of assessment can be difficult but much can be learned about the children's health, for example, simply by measuring their height and weight and comparing these with norms for their age. One can also build up a history of past and present illnesses.

The researchers will need to select the themes according to the target group and purpose of the study, but a comprehensive investigation on the impact of work on child development would include:

Physical development

☐ Rate of growth and development
☐ Nutrition
☐ Physical resilience
☐ Motor coordination
☐ Diseases

Intellectual development

☐ Linguistic and literacy skills
☐ Attention span
☐ Memory
☐ Cognitive ability
☐ Critical capacity
☐ Basic knowledge and understanding
☐ Numeracy

Socialization

☐ Degree and nature of personal interaction
☐ Culture and native language
☐ Adaptation to physical and social environment
☐ Access to mediums of socialization, e.g. family, school, etc.

Emotional development

☐ Personality development
☐ Affective capacity
☐ Feelings of self-esteem
☐ Values
☐ Attitudes about life
☐ Aspirations and feelings about the future

Religious and moral development

☐ Values concerning life and death
☐ Beliefs
☐ Moral code
☐ Religious beliefs

9.3. How children's circumstances have affected their family life

Family structure

☐ Household membership
☐ Family type (nuclear, single parent, step-family, extended, etc.)
☐ Household head/family leadership
☐ Number of siblings
☐ Child's position in birth order

Family support systems

☐ Quasi-familial relations (godparenthood, informal adoption/foster arrangements, etc.)

☐ Community groups and organizations (mothers' clubs, etc.)
☐ Religious organizations
☐ Government services
☐ Informal networks

Relations within the family

☐ Solidarity and reciprocity
☐ Intimacy
☐ Conflict

Physical conditions within the home

☐ Type/security of accommodation
☐ Size of living space and density of habitation
☐ Services
☐ Conditions of physical structure

9.4. How the economic situation of children and/or their families is affected by their circumstances

Income, capital and expenditure

☐ Forms of income (cash or kind)
☐ Sources of income
☐ Amount of income
☐ Distribution of resources within the household

Survival strategies

☐ Division of labour within the family

☐ Economic activities/occupations of family members (formal sector employment and informal activities)

☐ Economic roles of children

☐ Skills/knowledge/contacts of family members in labour market

☐ Employment opportunities

☐ Networks for barter or exchange

☐ Food aid and other donations

☐ Communal income-generating activities

9.5. The activities in which children are involved

Work

☐ Work histories

☐ Occupation

☐ Form/amount of payment

☐ Self-employed or wage earning

☐ Task/responsibilities

☐ Who benefits from wages

☐ Hours and conditions of work

☐ Attitudes to work

☐ Alternative sources of livelihood (gifts, barter, theft, begging, etc.)

Education

☐ Frequency of attendance at school

☐ Grade

☐ Interests at school

☐ Problems at school (learning, behavioural difficulties, etc.)

☐ Feelings about school

Recreation

☐ Amount of time given to recreation

☐ Recreative activities

☐ Companions during recreation periods

9.6. The circumstances of the community in which children live

Services and resources

☐ Health and sanitation

☐ Education

☐ Social/welfare services

☐ Housing

Communal organization

☐ Political and administrative structures

☐ Social groups/organizations

☐ Communal works

☐ Leadership (political, juridical, military)

Communication

☐ Radio or television transmission

☐ Newspapers, journals, books

☐ Transport (public and private, air, water, land)
☐ Telephone links

Economy

☐ Development agencies
☐ Market for production
☐ Management and business
☐ Incentives for economic growth
☐ Security of installations and equipment
☐ Availability of income for development

Relationship of children with their community

☐ Relations with the authorities, other children, local organizations and institutions, relatives and neighbours, etc.
☐ Participation in community events
☐ Involvement in community conflicts
☐ Community groups/individuals with whom children identify/from whom children gain support (emotional, economic, etc.)

9.7. How children feel about their situation

It is very important to explore the children's feelings about their situation. All too often, for example, adults have assumed that street children are distressed about their lives and circumstances. Sometimes the very opposite is true, since the children living on the streets may be the ones who have escaped oppression and abuse and chosen a life of independence and freedom. By offering children a chance to express their feelings on such issues, it may be possible to learn why they are in their present situation and what they hope, and expect, from the future.

CHAPTER SUMMARY

In any investigation of child labour there are a number of key themes or topics which can provide a framework. These include:
— *child development*;
— *the community context* — including the social relationships of children;
— *the range of child activities* — work, education and leisure;
— *the perceptions of children* of the past, present and future.

---

10. Summary and checklist on how to write a project document

10.1. Introduction

In Part II we explored the key concepts in project design and the linkages between them. In this final chapter we guide you through the writing of a summary project outline and a fully-fledged project document. The chapter concludes with a checklist to make sure that your proposal is clear, complete and consistent.

When you have an idea for a project, write it up first in the form of a Summary Project Outline (SPROUT) — see Box Thirteen. This will assist you in discussing and explaining your project idea with the relevant groups of people and organizations, including possible financing agencies. The preparation of a fully worked-out project document will usually be necessary as soon as a financing agency shows interest.

10.2. Project outline: Title page

— Project title.
— Tentative duration.
— Estimated starting date.
— Location.
— Project language.
— Main responsible agency.

— Other cooperating agencies.

— Donor contribution.

— Local contribution (specify in kind if necessary).

— Preparation date (in case of subsequent revisions, please indicate as follows: Revision 1, date; Revision 2, date, etc.).

A SUMMARY PROJECT OUTLINE (SPROUT)

A SPROUT must be concise and brief (suggested length about five pages). It consists of the following essential project components:

— *background and justification*, including a description of the identified *problem(s)*, the project's *strategy* to address the problem(s), the *target group(s)*, and the project's main *partners*;

— development and immediate *objectives*;

— main *outputs*;

— main *activities*;

— major *inputs*;

— *a preliminary budget estimate*.

The main differences between the fully-fledged project document and the SPROUT are:

— A project document contains separate and more detailed chapters on the *target group(s)* and the *institutional framework* or the partners associated with the project.

— A project document also contains chapters on:

— *indicators* of objective achievement;

— *assumptions* regarding the role of external factors;

— *reporting and evaluation*;

— *preconditions*;

— *budget*.

Within a SPROUT these additional chapters are not obligatory. However, they may be included if the project designer considers it necessary.

10.3. Project outline: A guide

Background and justification

(a) Describe in one or two paragraphs the general socio-economic situation in which the project will take shape.

(b) Describe the *problem(s)* to be addressed by the project.

(c) Describe the project *strategy*. What type of project interventions may be best suited to address the various aspects of the problem? *Direct support (DS)* projects aim to provide direct assistance to working children. *Institutional development (ID)* projects are concerned with strengthening the capability of an organization which works with, or on behalf of, children. Does the project use only one or does it combine both these approaches?

(d) Describe the major characteristics of the *target group(s)* or *intended beneficiaries* in terms of age, sex, and ethnic and social group. Pay specific attention to the situation of girls, who often get overlooked by project designers. Specify the target group(s):

Examples:

— children employed in specific industries;

— children working in the informal sector;

— children engaged in street trading;

— children working in agriculture;

— children engaged in domestic work;

— children engaged in prostitution;

— children confined in slave-like circumstances such as forced and bonded labour;

— children involved in hazardous occupations, e.g. mining and construction;

— any other category.

(e) Indicate the partners who will be involved in the project and their capability and potential to deliver services to working children.

(f) Projects work with a variety of intermediaries. In institutional development projects it is the staff of these organizations — NGOs, government agencies or community organizations — who will initially receive project benefits. They are the *direct recipients* of the project. Where this is the case, *describe how the project will ensure that the benefits resulting from the project will reach the target group.*

(g) Indicate the extent to which the partners, and particularly the intended beneficiaries, have been consulted in formulating the project.

(h) Describe the extent to which the project has incorporated lessons from earlier or ongoing activities in the problem area.

(i) Indicate the link of the project with the main international labour standards concerned with child labour. The following will be relevant:

— Is your country an ILO member State?

— Has the country ratified the Minimum Age Convention, 1973 (No. 138), or any of the relevant international labour Conventions relating to child labour?

— Consider whether the project could contain practical measures to promote these standards, e.g. through public awareness campaigns or training.

Development objective

The development objective describes the overall aim of the project. In child labour this is the protection of child workers and the long-term elimination of child labour. Describe how your project will contribute to this.

Immediate objective

An immediate objective is what the project hopes to achieve. It gives a picture of, or describes, the situation that is expected to prevail at the end of the project. Try to keep immediate objectives to a minimum, probably no more than three at most. Remember to be realistic and precise as far as possible. Your statement has to reflect the improvements which can be *directly attributed* to the outputs and activities of the project. Try to avoid using verbs such as "to study"; "to assist", "to discuss" or "to raise awareness". These describe activities rather than objectives, i.e. they are the means not the end:

— In a *DS project*, an immediate objective could be formulated as follows: "At the end of the project . . . per cent of children (identified by age, sex, class, location, etc.) will be removed from scavenging in . . . district and provided with basic education and training at . . .".

— In an *ID project*, an immediate objective could be formulated as follows: "At the end of the project the NGO . . . or Child Labour Unit of the Ministry of Labour will be capable of delivering . . . services to . . . target groups".

Outputs

These are the *products* which result from the project. Again, be precise. Examples are:

— X number of school places provided;

— X number of boys and girls provided with non-formal education;

— X number provided with skill training;

— X number benefiting from nutrition, health and other types of services, including protected work and shelter, etc.;

— X number of labour inspectors, government officials or NGO workers or volunteers trained;

— this or that type of study, report, manual, etc., prepared;

— this or that type of planning, coordinating structure established, e.g. child labour unit.

Activities

Activities transform inputs of the project into outputs. Give an overview of the project activities. This will help to explain and justify the request for specific resources. Examples are:

— training staff through workshops;

— preparing training manuals;

— carrying out surveys;

— developing curricula and materials;

— conducting advocacy campaigns;

— conducting seminars and conferences.

Inputs

Inputs are the resources needed to carry out the project. You also need to state who will be responsible for providing what. Inputs should be specified by:

— type;

— quantity;

— duration;

— cost.

For example, in an NGO project supported by an international financing agency:

Donor contribution:

(a) Technical expert (1) for 12 months, spread over three years at a total cost of $120,000.

(b) Training workshop for field workers, $20,000 per year (3) spread over three years.

(c) Equipment consisting of one computer, etc.

Local contribution:

In kind: office space, secretarial services, salaries of NGO staff (director, five field workers).

Indicators, assumptions and preconditions

In ID projects, indicators describe what the institution will be capable of doing. Example: "train X number of labour inspectors in child labour regulation".

In DS projects, indicators express to what extent the target group will be better off. Example: "the enrolment of primary aged children who were formerly child workers has increased by 30 per cent in region X".

Assumptions are factors beyond the control of the project management, which are important for the success of a project.

Preconditions are actions to be undertaken by the recipient organization in order to enable project activities to be carried out successfully.

Preliminary budget estimate

The calculation of the budget needs to be based on the list of inputs required to carry out the activities and on the prices and costs currently applicable in your country or project area. Give a budget estimate by year and in local currency or US dollars as convenient.

The main budget headings will be:

— personnel, including local travel, if any;

— subcontracts;

— training;

— equipment;

— miscellaneous, e.g. telephone, reporting costs.

10.4. A final checklist — Some useful hints

Having completed the project document, you need to go over it yourself (especially if it has been made by somebody else). If you drafted the project document yourself, you may also get others to check it for you to make sure that the proposal is complete and coherent, and worth undertaking. This is the project appraisal stage. Check in particular the *linkages* between the components, i.e. if the requested inputs are provided, the planned *activities* carried out and the *outputs* produced, is it likely that the stated *immediate objective(s)* will be achieved? You may find the following checklist helpful:

Background and context

Does this section reflect:

— identification of the project strategy, and an analysis of the child labour *problem(s)* to be addressed by the project;
— the analysis of alternative strategies and the justification for following the one proposed;
— how the project fits in with national priorities and strategies relating to child labour;
— how the project is related to international labour standards, e.g. Convention No. 138;
— how lessons learned in past child labour projects have been taken into consideration?

Target groups/partners

— Has the target group been identified precisely enough so that one can see later if it benefited?
— Have you identified the project partners and their capability?
— Have you clearly defined the approach of the project — ID, DS or both?
— In the case of an ID project, have the direct recipients been distinguished from the target group?

The development objective

— Has the immediate objective been formulated in such a way that there is a reasonable expectation that the project will make a contribution to it?

The immediate objective

Some tests to be applied:

— Is it really an objective rather than an activity or output?

— Does it reflect the primary strategy of the project, ID or DS?

Outputs

— Do they properly reflect the main strategy of the project?

— Are they necessary for achieving the immediate objective?

— Are they quantified and is it clear what will be produced by whom and when?

Activities

— Are the activities sufficient to produce the planned outputs?

— Has the timing been specified?

Inputs

— Are they all there, at the community, national and international levels?

— Have you been realistic about timing?

— Have you been realistic about the required qualifications of key personnel (an expert will usually not be a specialist in both child nutrition and advocacy)?

— Are funds for reporting and evaluation included in the budget?

Indicators

— Are the indicators precise enough to be used as criteria for the success of the project when it comes to evaluation?

— Will sufficient information be available so that measurable indicators can be formulated?

— Is data collection for indicators foreseen and is it linked to available baseline data?

Assumptions

— Have you specified *all* the external conditions that have to be satisfied for the project to achieve its objectives?

Preconditions

— Are you clear about the preconditions for the project to start, e.g. government support?

Monitoring and evaluation

— How will you monitor the progress of the project?

— What reports will be needed?

— How will you evaluate the effects of the project, and use the lessons in the future?

Budget

— Are the budget and the description of inputs consistent?

Bibliography

Bequele, A.; Boyden, J. (eds.). *Combating child labour* (Geneva, ILO, 1988).

Conditions of Work Digest (Geneva, ILO), Vol. 7, No. 1/1988, "The emerging response to child labour".

Idem, Vol. 10, No. 1/1991, "Child labour: Law and practice".

International Labour Office (ILO). *Procedures for the design and evaluation of ILO projects* (Geneva, 1981).

Idem. *Summary project outline (SPROUT): Guidelines for the preparation of summary project outlines for multi-bilateral financing* (Geneva, 1991).

Idem. International Programme on the Elimination of Child Labour (IPEC). Child Labour — *Problem analysis; formulation of action programmes: A compendium* (Geneva, 1992).

Myers, W. E. (ed.). *Protecting working children* (London and New Jersey, Zed Books/UNICEF, 1991).

United Nations Children's Fund (UNICEF). *Methodological guide on situation analysis of children in especially difficult circumstances* (Bogotá, 1988).

United Nations Development Programme (UNDP). *How to write a project document* (New York, 1990).